ALL SERVE TO SERVE!

"A Plan To Establish Strength Through Service For The United States!"

by

Dennis Andrew Ball,

author, THE BALL DOCTRINE:

"Creating Peace & Prosperity In Every Nation!"

Copyright © 2017 Dennis Andrew Ball

All rights reserved.

ISBN 13: 978-1975601119
10: 1975601114

<u>DEDICATION</u>

"THIS BOOK IS DEDICATED TO AMERICANS WHO SACRIFICE EVERYDAY TO PRESERVE PROTECT & DEFEND OUR LIBERTY AND FREEDOM FOR OUR CHILDREN AND GENERATIONS TO COME! NOW THE TIME HAS COME FOR A NEW GENERATION OF AMERICANS TO TAKE THE REIGNS OF STATE & MAKE THEM WORK AS THEIR OWN IN THE BEST INTERSTS OF THE PEOPLE, THEIR CHILDREN, THEIR FAMILIES AND GENERATIONS TO COME! SPECIAL THANKS DR. RICHARD D. HAGAN FOR HIS SUPPORT AND UNDERSTANDING OF THE TITLE

Dedication

Acknowledgment

Authors' Foreword

Notes
Appendix

1. ALL SERVE TO BE SERVED!   7

2. PRESIDENT KENNEDY.   13

3. THE PEACE DEPARTMENT.   17

4. MOS? Or COS? YOU DECIDE.   25

5. WHY NECESSARY?   30

6. STRENGTH THRU SERVICE.   32

7. CRISIS MANAGEMENT.   40

8. CIVILIAN SERVICE.   44

9. MILITARY SERVICE.   48

10. A TIME TO ACT!   52

ACKNOWLEDGEMENT

To The DEDICATION of Richard C. Hagan Demonstrated At A Time Of Great Danger To Our Nation During Uncertain Times In American History.

Author's Foreword

I am reminded by history past the history of the United States would not be complete if it were not for those gallant men and women who in the face of danger, proceeded to do something Special about it! This is the premise for **ALL SERVE TO SERVE: "A** *Plan To Establish Strength Through Service For The United States." Since the death of President Kennedy, events in America and the World have continued to show all of us how vulnerable our Nation is to crisis by man or nature and how our Citizenry & States of the United States should prepare in The*

BEST INTERESTS of ALL Americans.
ALL SERVE TO SERVE addresses the opportunities showing the way to fulfill the vision President Kennedy provided with a model by which America does its business to prepare for any eventuality brought to her shores. Strength through service is the prescription for all to serve their country either militarily or civilian, that President Kennedy envisioned.

1. *ALL SERVE TO BE SERVED!*
"A Nation That Serves Is A Nation Prepared"

The *history of America* would not be complete if it were not for the men and women who sacrificed so much of themselves for a new nation and its children. Of course, much can be said of those who plotted against them and used them to profit at their expense. For those they must answer for us we must correct their mistakes for our children and generations to come.

This then, becomes the back ground and back drop of *ALL SERVE TO SERVE: "A Plan To Establish Strength Through Service For The United States."*

"You cannot help the poor by destroying the Rich." "You cannot keep out of trouble by spending more than you earn." "You cannot lift the wage earner by pulling down the wage payer" – Abraham Lincoln

---

"I have always been afraid of banks."

"One man with courage makes a majority" "It is to be regretted that the rich & powerful too often bend the acts of government to their own selfish purposes." "Take time to deliberate but when the time for action arrives, stop thinking and go in." – *Andrew Jackson*

Let it be said, that America's finest hours are yet to come because the Children Of America can make a contribution to not only our Nation but also the World!

We are the product of generations past, present and future with the belief that our rights come from God; NOT THE STATE at a great cost to those who fought and died for them! That was the Social Contract created in 1781 at Yorktown-Gloucester Bay, Virginia.

The monuments laid at the reefs of those so honored are a testament to the sacrifice of so many for the hope that their sacrifice would *bear*. A proud nation was born and with it the greatest nation on earth in the history of mankind: "*AMERICA!*"

THE NATIONAL BACKGROUND

Early History

What was assumed by those in power was taken for granted by those struggling to live out their dreams. *AMERICA* was a land of opportunity because it's people made it their priority to continue living out their dreams for a better life for themselves and those for their children.

Colonial America grew at an astounding rate by the span of time from the founding of the Republic at Jamestown, Virginia 1607 until the last entry known as Georgia Colony 1732.

Of course, many events in between the time of founding and establishing Colonial life dominated the culture legally and politically;

particularly making it possible for 2.5 million people to realize their value because the Bible was read in the home, the schools and the Supreme Court! Ethics & Morales were also taught in the home practicing honesty and good business including honest services. The attitudes within the culture was fairness as the colonies grew in population and farming. As a result, the *Great Migration* ensued so that by the beginning of the War For Independence, *AMERICA* had enough population to fight England for it. And so we did on July 4, 1776 by way of the Declaration Of Independence, Congress, Philadelphia, Pennsylvania.

Now comes ALL SERVE TO SERVE redefining the current rules based on a *Socially Responsible* set of fundamental principles to meet human needs.

A responsive organizational means to protect , distribute, serve and preserve society as a whole. The concept of *Universal Service,*

What does it say and what does it mean?

We have here a system that creates a base of representation for sustainable, ethical, moral, and pragmatic means to the individual, family, community and greater society.

That is my point, unlike the history of *Early America* when life and government was much simpler and much smaller than now, we Americans did not have to deal with so much regulation and taxation without representation. Executive session was the oddity not common experience as is *today*.

Events do have a way of marking themselves to follow the outcome of what creates tremendous conflicts and tragedy in the lives of our Citizens and the outcome for our Children.

It is within this context that government *Of, By & For The People* will survive and thrive in this the twenty-first century and beyond.

ALL SERVE TO SERVE! is that vehicle

to get us there making old models obsolete.

WHAT are we talking about and HOW do we get there?

2. PRESIDENT KENNEDY
March 1, 1961 E.O.10924

"I am announcing today the formation of a new initiative for peace – The Peace Corp."

Shortly after his inauguration on January 20, 1961, President Kennedy's admonition to "Ask Not What Your Country Can Do For You But What You Can Do For Your Country", he announces the formation of the Peace Corps.

An initiative that still lives today founded on *his vision* known as *The New Frontier,* these programs to fight poverty, help cities, and expand governmental benefits to a wide array of Americans. His vision like that of this author, to intervene in the Third World to show America engaged in the daily struggles for national independence and sustainable solutions for the families of those nations.

Not socialism but free-enterprise capitalism, President Kennedy motivated by the adage "that a rising tide lifts all boats." His vision for an America with sustainability and that of his brother Bobby, both believed in the future of America & World and worked tirelessly to improve the quality of life for all The People.

As a consequence, Congress saw value in supporting and funding the "Peace Corps" as an integral functioning part of the United States government in countering communism during the 'Cold War' to keep it becoming a 'Hot War' & commissioned its establishment shortly after it was introduced in committee.

This was a prelude to American Foreign Policy that attempted to keep America out Of Third World conflicts by showing them America was invested in their success. This policy is consistent with that introduced by THE BALL DOCTRINE: "Creating Peace & Prosperity In Every Nation." amazon.com

Now the question remains, why is this important and how do we get to where we are going?

As the title of this book portrays, service in support of society's 'Strategic Interests' the time has come to rethink what life in America could be to both set the example of Citizen participation & preparedness for emergency's under the umbrella of *Universal Service.*

But in a broader and greater sense, the duty and engagement of the population to create from within itself the attitude of *compulsive service* by which the security interests of the United States are affirmed by citizenry that chooses to support it.

Eligibility for both men and women from ages 16-30 years for both military and civilian occupational service including active reserve would assist in their education and ability to fund after leaving their respective services.

Those services include Peace Corps,

Americorps, Conservation Corps and Health & Human Services on civilian side; Army, Navy, Marines, Air Force, Coast Guard for military. These are the conduits for our people to engage themselves in creating a nation STRONG in defending her vital interests and keeping her families safe from any eventuality that threatens the wellbeing of the nation.

What is coming forth to empower our nation is 'strength through service' and a plan to make that happen.

3. THE PEACE DEPARTMENT

"Blessed Are The Peace Makers For They

Shall Be Called The Children Of God"

Matthew 5: 9

"Do we dare ever ask the right

questions pertaining to War & Peace?

Former Congressman (D) Ohio,

Dennis John Kucinich

As a candidate for President of the

United States, I am constantly reminded by

the solemn duty our men and women in the

uniform of the United States place their lives

in the cross hairs of danger every single day.

I must say that is consistent for all of us

who believe in the Vanguard of the Nation.

The Core Kernel of Social Benefits for a

COMMON DEFENSE either militarily or

civilian with a dimension of service that

creates preparedness for the nation in times of crisis either man made or by that of nature including War & Peace.

Intergenerational code of conduct based on social, economic and ecological needs. Creating the means to support the ends to find both a way to prepare America in times of crisis and also make a way for Peace to be created for by those serving abroad in the Peace Corp.

In other words, a strategy for society in terms to multiplicate to meet the minimum for High Profile situations with troop strength including active reserve.

But to a greater degree, the benefits out pace one's duty to one's country and oneself to be prepared for any eventuality that may come to harm or damage our nation.

The need for specialists in the fields of

Medicine, Bio-technology, Science, Math, Technical Schools, Skilled Labor Education, Vo-tech in preparation for one to receive either a high school diploma or their GED to pursue courses that will assist their education and begin the process of building character and independence in the Best Interests of the family and the nation.

Why is this important for the Department Of Peace?

From here the ambitions of many maybe realized by those within its base of support; primarily those actively seeking their degree programs be it Bachelors, Masters, Phd, MD, Juris Doctorate –JD, giving rise to a Civil Service Corps. adequately supplied with necessary personnel that also can assist for Veterans issues within the Veterans Administration and the Science of

Agricultural innovation and production like Osmotic Tubing.

You do your 2 years of compulsive military or civilian service, you receive 2 years of credit for your service. If you wish to stay longer up to 4 years, you receive as a benefit 4 years of college tuition to complete your education debt free. This is also good for technical schools to prepare for a trade.

Aptitude, Interest & Ability are core to making our society work for the family's Best Interests. After all, our nation is only as good as our people demonstrate attitudes that reflect good will and preparation for its survival and sustainability. Virtues that are also indicative of a nation at peace versus a nation in perpetual war.

It is time to give Peace a chance and with it the core values that make America a great nation! Peace through strength; not weakness must be become our strategic montra to change the direction of our culture and our future. For too long, we have been hostages to a corporate elite making the rules and breaking the rules at our expense.

Today, that stops! We are Americans by The American Party Of America! Our goals are simple and mission is clear. We cannot afford to have people in place who abuse the Constitution, abuse us, and make life more difficult while the same they use our money and property to profit at our expense. This is white collar crime and this is wrong!

Therefore, to implement this task, we ask of our inductees to prepare themselves to take an eight week program of training to learn the basics of Universal Service either within the military or civilian service. These are the building blocks for Peace through Strength to make our society strong again and prepare the nation for any eventuality.

Within the military branches of service are the Army, Navy, Air Force, Marines, Coast Guard including Active Reserve which entitles a Lifetime profession and full health benefits. This makes it possible for young people to get their education paid for by committing at least 2 years or 4 years of active military service to their country with little or no debt coming out of their chosen fields

This applies equally to Civilian Service: The Peace Corp., Americorp, Conservation Corp,, Health & Human Service Corp. To train young people in disciplines to assist them in transitioning to job skills to make a living wage. That is BALLONOMIC$,

"Lifting America & The World Out Of Poverty From The Bottom Up!" by Dennis Andrew Ball, amazon.com.

The Department of Peace as structured as a Cabinet level executive branch reporting to the President of The United States; also serving on the National Security Council.

The position as defined would cause both The Secretaries Of State & Defense to consult with the Peace Secretary when conflicts are about to start for non-violent means of conflict resolution.

It would also fund 'Stop The Violence Programs" in cities and schools with an unarmed civilian peace keeping contingent.

It would sponsor its own Peace Academy modeled after military service academies. After 4 years, graduates spend 5 years in Public service promoting non-violence conflict resolution at home or abroad.

Finally, it would sponsor "Peace Day" held everywhere discussion in professional activities and achievements in the lives of peacemakers.

That my friends is a $10 Billion dollar a year government agency well worth its weight to save the tax payer money and avoid costly expense of lives & resources. It is also consistent with the Best Interests of the family aka THE BALL DOCTRINE!

4. *MOS? Or COS? YOU DECIDE*

The notion of Universal Service is not New to the national dialogue. What is different are the times by which the subject is being raised.

For centuries dating back to 1793, the Introduction of a Peace Department came about because of an essay titled "A Plan Of A Peace Office For The United States." by Dr. Benjamin Rush, a signer of the Declaration of Independence. Since then, many bills were introduced but none passed the mustered of today's date and time. It is time for it to come and become a part of the dialogue in everyday America & World.

As was with President Kennedy, his vision for America included pragmatic initiatives & solutions dealing with complex problems improving the quality of life for our Citizens and generations to come. How he was able to establish the means to support the ends and keep America Strong as a force for good in the World is the legacy he left us to build. Both he and his brother, Robert Kennedy had dreams and visions for the American people that was slowed but not defeated because of what they did during the time they lived.

Like all Americans, we are a Motley Crew of diverse backgrounds and race but all belong to the family of the human race. This there in lays the challenge of our democracy and our freedoms to *make* them strong for our children & generations to come. How we do that will determine the outcome of what we do now to strengthen our society and *keep* it strong.

Military or Civilian Service to one's Country is a good start! Why? Because Strength Through Service mirrors the skills necessary to employ in times of crisis. Those times demand a preparedness to assist our people despite the gloom and doom of the moment.

America as a nation and We as a People require that our nation be United in the service for *her* Children. Why? Anything less, would be *Uncivilized.* Tearing down America has no place amongst our people. Building her up has every opportunity to *building* and *keeping* her safe and strong.

Compulsive Military or Civilian Service is necessary for our young people to build character and show their peers disciplined leadership in establishing themselves in the working dynamics of national preparedness.

Our *hope* is to breath new life into *our Society* by causing our young people to get educated in disciplined skills, service to one's Country and putting families first in business, labor and government.

For too long, we have been coddled and lied too about our *history* and our *freedoms.* We are a nation of proud people molded in the finest traditions that mankind has known. That does not mean that abuse has not gotten in the way. That is what *must* be corrected.

Anything less, would be *Uncivilized!* To create the different corps. for young people to invest demands choices that fit for their interests, aptitudes and abilities.

In the *Appendix,* a Universal Service chart shows the choices available to take the opportunity to enlist in a program that interests you and supports your aptitudes and abilities.

This is your opportunity to give back to a nation that needs your talents, skills and abilities to give back to her children and generations to come and create the preparedness necessary to support our families and their future!

5. WHY NECESSARY?

The most obvious is for young people to make better decisions and go into life debt free.

"I CAN!" "I WILL!" I am determined! That job out there you want is at your finger tips. All you have to do is go get it! Your choices are at your command with the skills and abilities you possess! Let the World know you are here to do a job that pays you for your skills that are needed to make money for you.

An escrow account can make you happy! How? For every year you invest in yourself you build an equity like in a GI Bill.

If you invest yourself in the military services, you receive in your account time served with skill deployment to contribute to your education once you leave serving your country. Same for Civilian Service.

What is your plan? Sit down & write it down! What are your Goals? These are questions that must be asked to assist you in making these decisions.

Active duty reserves also pays you dividends and can assist you and the nation in times of crisis. But it also creates attitudes of preparedness through service for the sake of our children and their families. That is important!

You can also prepare for retirement by making contributions depending if you stay in the military or civilian service.

6. STRENGTH THRU SERVICE

Ultimately, our goal to create a society of functionally literate citizens ready, willing & able to respond to any crisis in a timely and effective manner.

These goals also contain elements where attitudes are made that keep us safe & cause us to support our neighbor as a way of life of becoming good citizens.

When we *serve* each other and make that our life's mission, we are fulfilling our role to our children and grand children. They see in us what maybe missing within themselves.

Now is the time to become engaged in doing what must be done; that is serving "The Greater Good."

How does one do it? How do we make

a difference in the lives of parents & kids?
I'm reminded by examples from others who
sacrificed themselves so that others might be
free. Now, we are facing a conscience crisis
affecting every aspect of our lives. This was
very evident in the early 60's and continues
now more than ever.

Movement's begin when people know
their lives and those of their children are
at risk. Abraham Lincoln compared it to
the living making a more perfect Union
in his Gettysburg Address November 19,
1863.

I compare it to taking responsibility
for the actions of family members who wish
to violate the safety and security of the other
members. This is a huge problem created by
years of both privilege and neglect for lack

of knowledge or the will to exercise it!

How can this be you ask? How can it not be is the answer. Why? If We The People are not working in the BEST INTERESTS of our family, *whose* interests are we working fore? The individual good? The collective good of society? Both?

Again, I am reminded by examples of others who sacrificed and sacrifice for their neighbors to know them and make their lives better. This is the collective good I believe President Kennedy was well on his way of establishing especially in his books known as *"PROFILES IN COURAGE", "WHY ENGLAND SLEPT"; "A NATION OF IMMIGRANTS"*.

From humble beginnings the adage 'Strength Through Service" gained momentum. President Kennedy knew what it meant to not only serve but to risk one's life in the service of your country!

Brave men who give themselves facing difficult problems show all of us what it means to be a soldier and an American!

Let us always remember the sacrifices for us by those who fought for us and our Freedoms. Let us remember the price they paid for us to be free and for us to repay them by staying free.

Our children will thank us and their children from the legacy we leave so that they may be free from the examples that are demonstrated everyday by citizens in neighborhoods and communities that value what is and what can.

"WE CAN!""WE WILL!" do what must

be done to make *"America strong again!"*

Compulsive service teaches young people discipline and provides structure for their lives that assists the Best Interests of both society and that of the family unit.

Children need to know they are valued and important and that society cares about their mental and physical wellbeing.

Families impacted by divorce are victims of a negligent and abusive culture that keeps creating the conditions by which the break up of the home is sustained by the very people responsible for its demise. Who are they? Your neighbors, Your City Council, Your Mayors, Governors even your own family and extended family. How? Why?

Churches who espouse faith in God but miss the mark in holding up the Best

Interests of the family, share in the abuse and neglect that government creates by mothers separate themselves from fathers for money AFDC/TANF or parents who find their children separated from them by CPS foster care parents by Title IV-E **Adoption & Safe Families Act (ASFA).** This act was created by Hillary Rodham Clinton signed into law by her husband, Bill Clinton resulting in the absconding of thousands if not millions of children into foster care since 1997. For every child placed, the State receives money from the federal government to go into their general fund.

We hear nothing from Governors of the United States demanding an end to this practice nor that of nursing home abuse by State Court Guardianships. America has much dirty laundry regarding family abuse by State governments by all three branches.

Let us decide NOW! this will change for our children and generations to come. The abuse must stop and normalcy return to the land of plenty. Our hopes and dreams can be fulfilled once we align ourselves with policies and procedures conducive for them.

Strength comes by serving others because the idea is once we serve we too are served by a culture of service WE create for ourselves and for others. It starts with us, the citizens of these United States.

Again, this I believe was the vision of John F. Kennedy and his brother, Bobby. Both men were in touch with these issues of sacrifice and service to one's country. They spoke of it in their homes and lived it in their lives. They were a shining example of a City on a Hill. A shining light for all to see and comprehend. Their time has passed while ours has just begun. Let's make it count and *make* and *keep* our nation Strong!

7. CRISIS MANAGEMENT

"How do you manage a Crisis?"

"One Problem At A Time."

Do we have the 'Will & Skill' to take responsibility for problems in our *society* that impact us personally? Is the rate of change in *society* making it more difficult for our citizens to function normally? Can we find answers to assist us in the growing epidemic of complex problems plaguing our lives and making them more difficult to survive and thrive? The answers lay with We The People for this chapter is dedicated.

I am constantly reminded of our past as a nation and society and how our heritage dealt with establishing and maintaining their lives. Now, it is our turn to make the frontier land become the land of the frontier whereby knowledge replaces dogma, policy replaces dictum and creativity establishes the means to support the ends within the middle class.

Our nation "CAN!" & "WILL!" fight to Preserve, Protect & Defend Citizen's Rights by the Constitution of these United States making it a priority.

Also making it a crime to substitute any form of subversion with another cultures' law replacing our own.

Society must understand the stakes for inaction are greater than those for fear of taking action against all threats both foreign and domestic. Society has a duty to respond and act in the Best Interests of the family because do otherwise would be *uncivilized.*

Our allegiance comes from our faith in

God and our understanding that guides us.
A moral people is required to hold an
immoral government accountable who uses
its citizens' as pawns and parrots feeding off
their labor and their money.

I have preached it since 2011 of Taxation
Without Representation coming out against
Big Government & Big Spending in
AMERICA 2000: "Foundations For
Generations!" (amazon.com) & video
segments on Youtube –Dennis Andrew Ball.

Holding others accountable is job one for
Citizens that care about their children,
themselves and generations to come.

Doing it begs this question:

"If you are not working in the BEST
INTERESTS of your family, whose interests
are you working fore?" In times of crisis, all

options should be on the table to survive and thrive within the rule of law. Neglect and indecision are anathema to preparedness and success. Indeed, all of us make up a part of our community but how many of us are prepared and ready to engage the enemy or worse, know what to do in an emergency for children and ourselves?

This is why ALL SERVE TO SERVE has relevance for the times we live. It also makes sense that *society* has a responsibility to protect its children and provide for them what is necessary for their survival. Only then will we be prepared to handle any eventuality thrown at us.

Public safety is paramount and creating the means to make that happen is too. Our priorities should be to our families safety.

8. CIVILIAN SERVICE

The 8 weeks of compulsive training to prepare us for service to our Country either in military or civilian are common to all.

That training is boot camp regardless of your branch of choice. Common to all is the preparation to invest yourself in the security of your country and the world. Showing the discipline you exude to keep us safe from threats both domestic and foreign is the trademark of being an American.

Engaging oneself in facing down the enemies of *liberty* and *freedom* means that *justice* is relevant and necessary for our times. It means we can Keep America Strong making her that "City on a Hill" for all to see and adopt!

Behavioral development that puts others

first accounting for one's actions & deeds, needs be foundational for the time spent preparing to do a special job defending the Republic of these United States and making the families of these United States secure in the knowledge and actions of her people.

This training includes weapons, first-aid including first responders to on-scene issues that grip the community or nation; Survival skills that assist in support of life saving of other people within your community/nation.

It may also lead to advance training with active reserve within a military component. These components maybe interchangeable applying to one or both. The goal leading the nation to independence by our own people in preparedness for any eventuality life wishes to create for us.

Career options relates to the value of choosing between Military Occupational Services or Civilian Occupational Services. Both have their advantages for the time one invests themselves.

Funding for both comes from entitlement programs funded by government initiatives. A portion by which is invested in the futures of our youth and their Best Interests.

It is estimated that enrollments in these Federally mandated programs would be distributed with 60% into military the other 40% into civilian services.

They would act as a buffering agent against problems that would potentially overwhelm our nation and provide support & protection against all threats both foreign and domestic.

This then becomes the model and future for our youth. Programs that teach learning skills preparing for disaster relief, how to handle a weapon; how to prepare for crisis intervention; how to run to the fire opposed to abandoning it. Basic first-aid & survival skills.

One may decide to make these programs a career or be challenged by a private life of one's own including going into business for oneself. All of these options are available to the person who has prepared themselves to face their future head-on with courage and determination.

These are the qualities of a prepared & strong nation both emotional and economic. Strength through Service provides a positive future for the youth of the United States!

9. MILITARY SERVICE

As has been discussed, we are at a cross Roads in our nation to prepare ourselves for any eventuality. President Kennedy said "A rising tide lifts all boats" & "We go to the moon not because its easy but because it is hard."

Our heritage as a nation demands we pay the price for freedom meaning every man, woman and child participating in protecting the nation and the reality of it. Our Bill Of Rights, to a large measure is dependent on Courts and Judges who follow and uphold the tenants and statues placed before them excusing themselves from making law by actions adverse to those they take an Oath to protect.

Our security to our future is tied to our

investment in our youth and how we as a nation listen and learn to the promises we make to their service.

If you do two years you get two years in an escrow account. Four for four. Five and more depending upon your level of interest including National Guard.

The military component of ALL SERVE TO SERVE is designed to modernize and mobilize the nation in times of peace and war. Both have their place in the context of preparedness. Both require strong family support. Both need the nation's blessing.

We are a proud nation with a rich history of military service. Our freedoms are a result of our soldiers and families sacrifices for the children of America & generations to come.

Can we do any less for those who gave

their all? Beginning Falls Church, Virginia 1775 plotting against the British government with their grievances, our nation has always responded from the injustice within. Can it be any different today? Should we not be vested as they who identified a problem & did something positive about it?

Military service provides Discipline and Structure in the service of one's country. Both are essential to maintaining a "free" People under the United States Constitution.

Serving one's country has it's advantages and makes it possible for society to maintain our freedoms and liberty by being prepared for any eventuality.

ALL SERVE TO SERVE means ALL SERVE TO BE SERVED! The magic of these words are that the nation is prepared to fight against an enemy that may be seen or not seen. A threat that cannot be ignored and a future created of uncertainty by a nation ill prepared to handle it. That must be our mission to solve and our goal as a people.

If we dedicate ourselves to the future of our children and their Best Interests, then we will fulfill our mission of Universal Service to all and we in turn will be served by those we served in the "duty" of citizenship.

Our history as a nation implores us to reach out become one's neighbor & prepare ourselves to act when "duty" calls. This is the legacy our ancestors left us can we do no less? I leave the answer with all of you.

America is only as strong as her families requiring all to participate in her defense.

10. A TIME TO ACT!

In the course of history, our nation has faced many threats to its security and our freedoms all of which all of us owe a great debt of gratitude to those who sacrificed it all for us!

Can we do no less than to preserve, protect and defend our nation and our Children? Did they not do that for us?

Let us not be selfish and let us decide to act in our nations families Best Interests. Let us not tarry long with that which must get done!

ALL SERVE TO SERVE is:

ALL SERVE TO BE SERVED by making priority compulsive military or civilian service in the defense of our country so that in turn we are all beneficiaries of our nation.

NOTES

APPENDIX

U.S. National Universal Service
All Serve to Be Served - A Nation That Serves Is a Nation Prepared

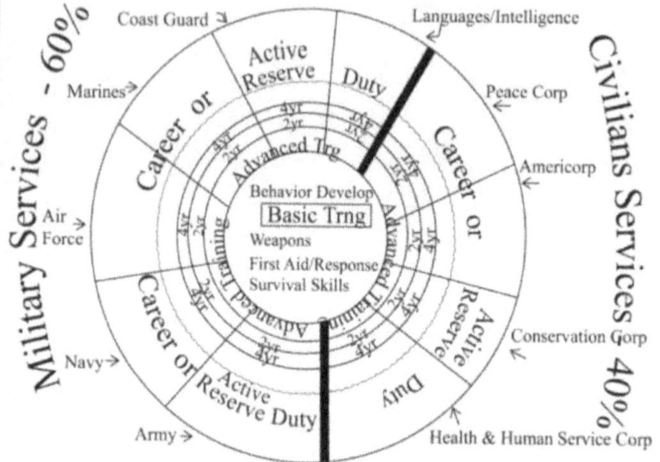

Key Elements

1. Ages of Eligibility - 16 thru 30, No race, gender
2. Education for Service - 2 for 2/4 for 4/5 Reserve or Career Master's+
3. Military Service and A Civilian Service
4. Career Options relate to MOS and a COS. Some may interchangeable
5. Funding Military plus Percentage vof Entitlements.
6. Funds for Education - Salaries % held in Escrow or from Advancement by promotion, time in grade on length of service